IMAGES
of Scotland

AIRDRIE

From Left to right: James Glidden, Marion Glidden, Helen Moir, Bill Moir.

Acknowledgements

I would like to thank the following people who have helped in the compilation of this book. They are the staff at the *Airdrie & Coatbridge Advertiser*; Fiona McNair, John Henderson, Mary Duckett of Larkhall, Percy and Janice lafferty, Gina and Robert Cowan, Cllr Andrew Burns of Bargeddie & Langloan. This book would not have been possible without them. I'd also like to thank Campbell McCutcheon for the image on the cover.

IMAGES
of Scotland

AIRDRIE

Helen Moir

TEMPUS

First published 2001

Tempus Publishing Limited
The Mill, Brimscombe Port,
Stroud, Gloucestershire, GL5 2QG
www.tempus-publishing.com

ISBN 0 7524 2368 1

Typesetting and origination by
Tempus Publishing Limited
Printed in Great Britain by
Midway Colour Print, Wiltshire

The Airdrie & Coatbridge Tramway COMPANY.

TO OR FARES. FROM

			Fare	Colour of Ticket.
Woodside St.	and	Manse St.	½D.	White.
Manse St.	and	Fountain		
Fountain	and	Jackson St.		
Jackson St.	and	Coatdyke.		
Coatdyke	and	Ralston St.		
Ralston St.	and	Airdrie Station		
Airdrie Cross	and	Motherwell St.		
Woodside St.	and	Jackson St.	1D.	Red.
Manse St.	and	Coatdyke		
Fountain	and	Ralston St.		
Jackson St.	and	Airdrie Station		
Coatdyke	and	Motherwell St.		
Woodside St.	and	Coatdyke	1½D.	Blue.
Manse St.	and	Ralston St.		
Fountain	and	Airdrie Station		
Jackson St.	and	Motherwell St.		
Woodside St.	and	Airdrie Station	2D.	Green.
Manse St.	and	Motherwell St.		
Woodside St.	and	Motherwell St.	2½D.	Salmon.

WORKMEN'S FARES.

For each 1d. Stage, ½d. Colour of Ticket Cerise. | Through Fare, 1d. Colour of Ticket. Lilac.

CHILDREN'S FARES.

The Fare to be charged for Children between the ages of 3 and 12 years will be as follows:— 1d. Colour of Ticket. Orange.
Between Woodside Street, Coatbridge, and Motherwell Street, Airdrie,
Halfpenny Fare Stages as per above Fare List. The Company reserve the right to discontinue this Special Fare at any time without notice.

Each passenger shall on demand pay to the Conductor or other duly authorised officer of the Company on the Car the fare legally demandable for the journey.

Passengers are respectfully requested to observe that the Conductor punches in their presence a Ticket for the Section to be travelled over, representing the value of the fare paid.

Tickets are only available for the journey, and on the Car on which issued.

Passengers must retain their Tickets for inspection by the Company's Officials, or give them up on demand, if required.

The Directors request the assistance of the Public in carrying out the Regulations of the Company.

PERIODICAL REVISION OF FARES.

Tram fares, 1910. The trams have long gone and been replaced by a plethora of buses.

Contents

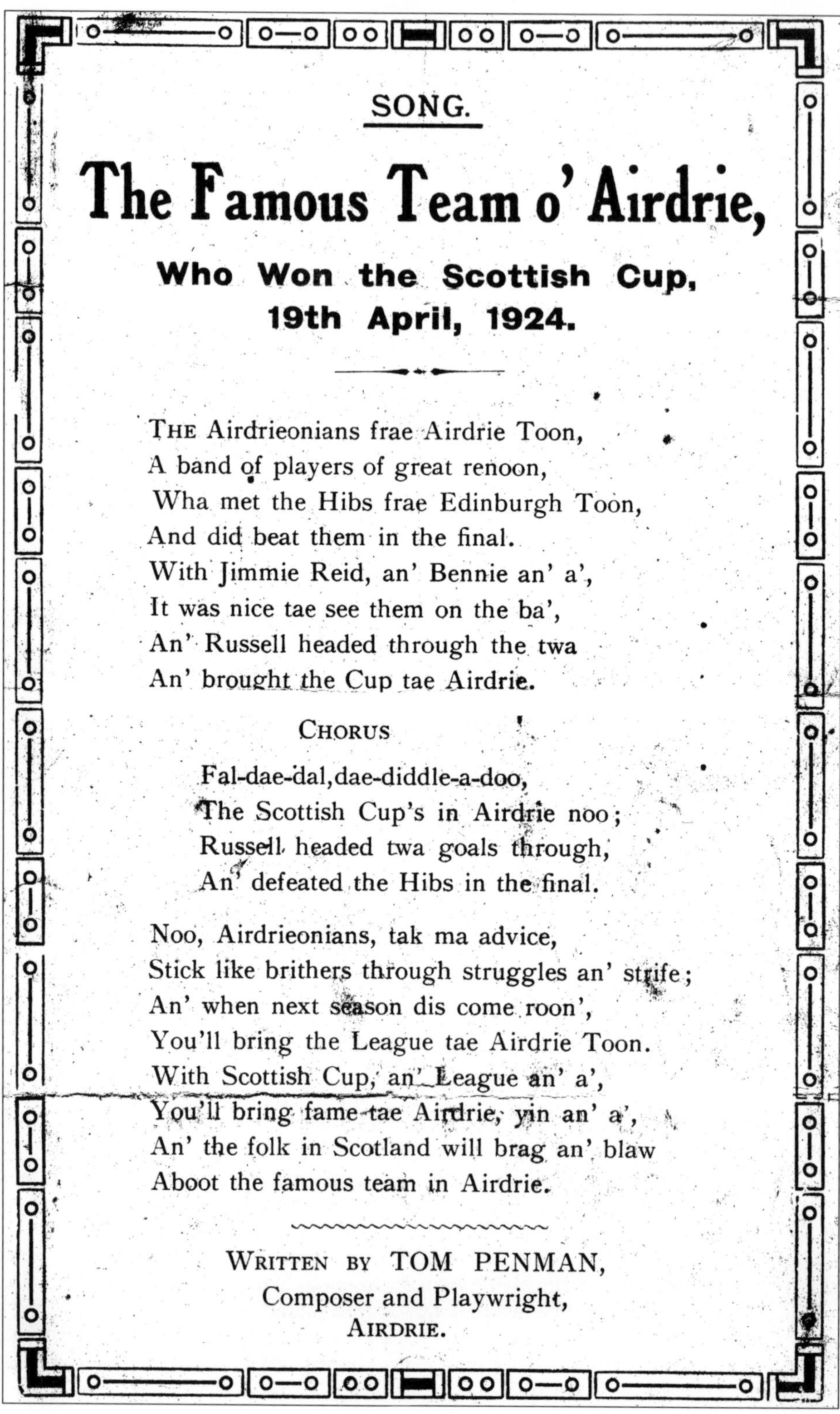

SONG.

The Famous Team o' Airdrie,

Who Won the Scottish Cup, 19th April, 1924.

THE Airdrieonians frae Airdrie Toon,
A band of players of great renoon,
Wha met the Hibs frae Edinburgh Toon,
And did beat them in the final.
With Jimmie Reid, an' Bennie an' a',
It was nice tae see them on the ba',
An' Russell headed through the twa
An' brought the Cup tae Airdrie.

CHORUS

Fal-dae-dal, dae-diddle-a-doo,
The Scottish Cup's in Airdrie noo;
Russell headed twa goals through,
An' defeated the Hibs in the final.

Noo, Airdrieonians, tak ma advice,
Stick like brithers through struggles an' strife;
An' when next season dis come roon',
You'll bring the League tae Airdrie Toon.
With Scottish Cup, an' League an' a',
You'll bring fame tae Airdrie, yin an' a',
An' the folk in Scotland will brag an' blaw
Aboot the famous team in Airdrie.

WRITTEN BY TOM PENMAN,
Composer and Playwright,
AIRDRIE.

Introduction

The area around Airdrie has been settled for thousands of years and evidence of occupation by both the Romans and the tribes that preceded them is to be found within the vicinity of the town. Roman forts and roads are nearby and artifacts such as coins have been found over the years.

In AD 577 the battle of Arderyth was fought somewhere in the vicinity when the army of Rydderech defeated Aidan the Perfidious, King of Cantyre. The Celtic poet Merlin was awarded a golden torc for his celebratory verses despite being on the losing side.

In 1160 King Malcolm IV gave the land of the area to the monks of Newbattle in a charter of that year. The industrious monks improved the land, much of which was marsh and scrub and kept sheep over much of the area, with the wool being exported as far away as the Low Countries. The principal residence for the monks was at Drumpellier although they had outlying settlements elsewhere, for example at Kipps and Chapelhall. The monks also built mills and had a meal mill at Airdrie. They improved communications between their lands at Newbattle and the Monklands. The road that connected their lands eventually became the main Edinburgh to Glasgow road. In 1795 the road became the Glasgow-Edinburgh turnpike road and came through Airdrie from the west via Cliftonhill and Airdrie House. It then passed through High Street, Bridge Street, Hallcraig, Flowerhill, and Colliertree. It was along this road that the first houses in Airdrie were built.

Until 1695 the town remained essentially a small farm hamlet with only a few houses. In that year Robert Hamilton gained a charter giving the town burgh status, entitling it to hold markets and charges customs dues for goods imported into the town. A weekly market and four annual fairs could be held. The population of the town were employed in candle making, weaving and distilling. It was weaving that was to become one of the largest industries in the town and many hand loom weavers lived here in mainly thatched single storey houses. Hand loom weaving declined after the end of the Napoleonic Wars for two reasons, one was the lessening of demand for cloth from the military and the other was mechanisation. New power mills were being introduced in other parts of the county, most notably at New Lanark.

Airdrie's main industry in the nineteenth century was coal mining. Coal was known in the area from medieval times but it was the nineteenth century when a rapid expansion of mining took place. Coal, ironstone and fireclay were all mined locally and the area underneath the town became riddled with mine workings. The rapid growth of the industry also saw a huge increase in the town's population. Much of the coal and ironstone that was mined was destined for the ironworks of nearby Coatbridge and Airdrie residents could often not look down on their neighbour as Coatbridge was covered in a pall of smoke and pollution from the many works.

In the nineteenth century the town had many benefactors, the most well known being Sir John Wilson who lived in Airdrie House. He donated the public park which was opened on 19 November 1897. Its opening commemorated Queen Victoria's diamond jubilee of that year. A bandstand was erected also. In 1908 he laid out West End park and donated it to the town as well. He died in 1918.

As well as the main Edinburgh-Glasgow road the canal came to the town in the late eighteenth century when James Watt engineered the Monkland Canal. The canal was used to transport coal and iron to Glasgow and export to the rest of the world. It has now been filled in along much of its route in and around the town. Railways came to the area in the 1820s and the Monkland & Kirkintilloch Railway was the first of many to criss-cross the Monklands.

Airdrie can also be proud of its sporting tradition. It has a good football team in the Diamonds as well as a fine boxing tradition, some of which can be seen in the forthcoming pages.

A school group at Chapelside School, *c.*1930.

One
Airdrie People

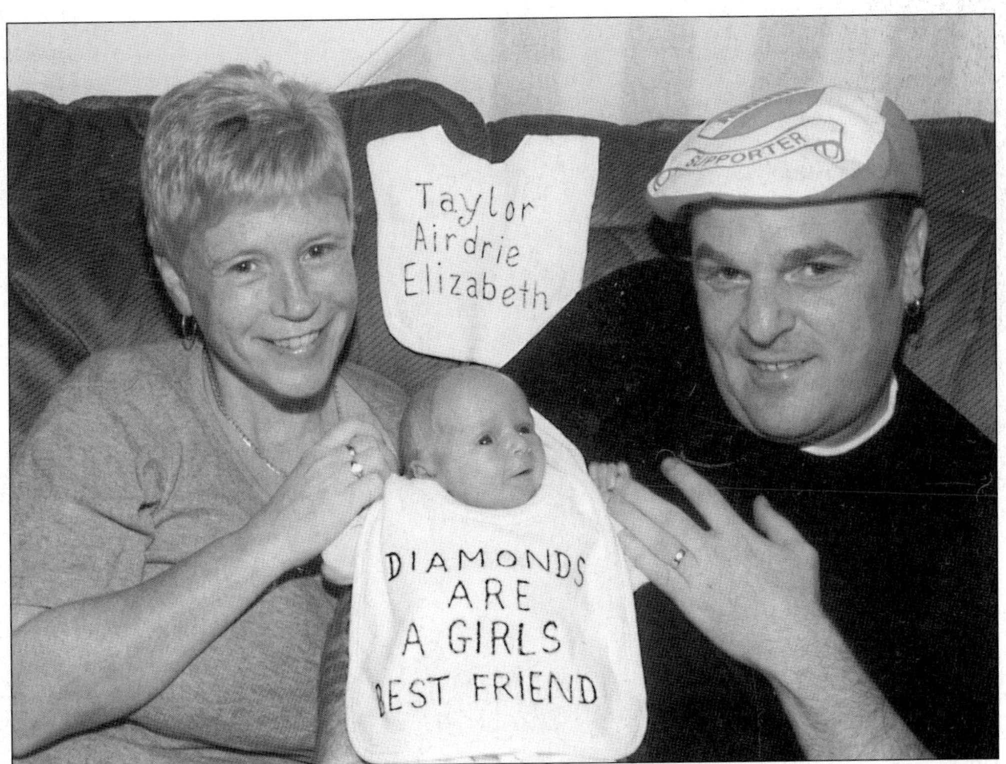

Named after her father's favourite football team, this is Taylor Airdrie Elizabeth Beslom. Her proud dad Eric is a keen supporter of the Diamonds. (Photograph courtesy Airdrie & Coatbridge Advertiser).

The kids of Alexandra Primary School after raising a whopping £2,000 for Holy Childhood. Father Isaac McLaren picked up the cheque on behalf of the church charity after the pupils at the Airdrie school had spent all of 1999 collecting. (Photograph courtesy Airdrie & Coatbridge Advertiser).

Here are the staff at Colston Garage, Carlisle Road, who collected £725 for Children in Need. From left to right are Gail Wilson, Moira Morrisey and Trisha Johnston. (Photograph courtesy Airdrie & Coatbridge Advertiser).

Bookworms at Airdrie Academy raised £1,300 for the Readathon Charity by being sponsored to read as many books as possible in a week. Airdrie Academy rector Hugh MacCallum and teacher Isabel Randall are pictured here with the pupils. (Photograph courtesy Airdrie & Coatbridge Advertiser).

Calderbank school pupils triumph in North Lanarkshire's schools quiz. The kids from Corpus Christi Primary were the winners of 118 teams from North Lanarkshire primary schools. The final was at Bellshill Cultural Centre and Provost Barry McCulloch presented the prizes. The winning team was Anthony McGoldrick, Christopher Donnelly, Sarah Bolland, Louise Clark and Stephen Carr. (Photograph courtesy Airdrie & Coatbridge Advertiser).

These Carnbroe Primary kids got a taste of the orient when they entered poems in the National Museum of Scotland's Enter the Dragon competition. The aim was to help Scots and Chinese children respect each other's religions and cultures. Primary 6 entered poems about Chinese dragons, ranging in style from funny to sad. Kim Stevenson and Carolyn Grant (centre) represented the school in the prize giving ceremony and read out the poems. (Photograph courtesy Airdrie & Coatbridge Advertiser).

Blowing your own trumpet...that's what the pupils of Airdrie Academy were doing in 2001 when they raised £600 for the St Andrew's Hospice in Airdrie. (Photograph courtesy Airdrie & Coatbridge Advertiser).

The Girl Can't Help It is showing at the New Cinema, Broomknoll Street, in 1956 and here is Ida Brown, the cashier and receptionist at the cinema, pictured on the right. The building was demolished in 1980. (Photograph courtesy John Henderson).

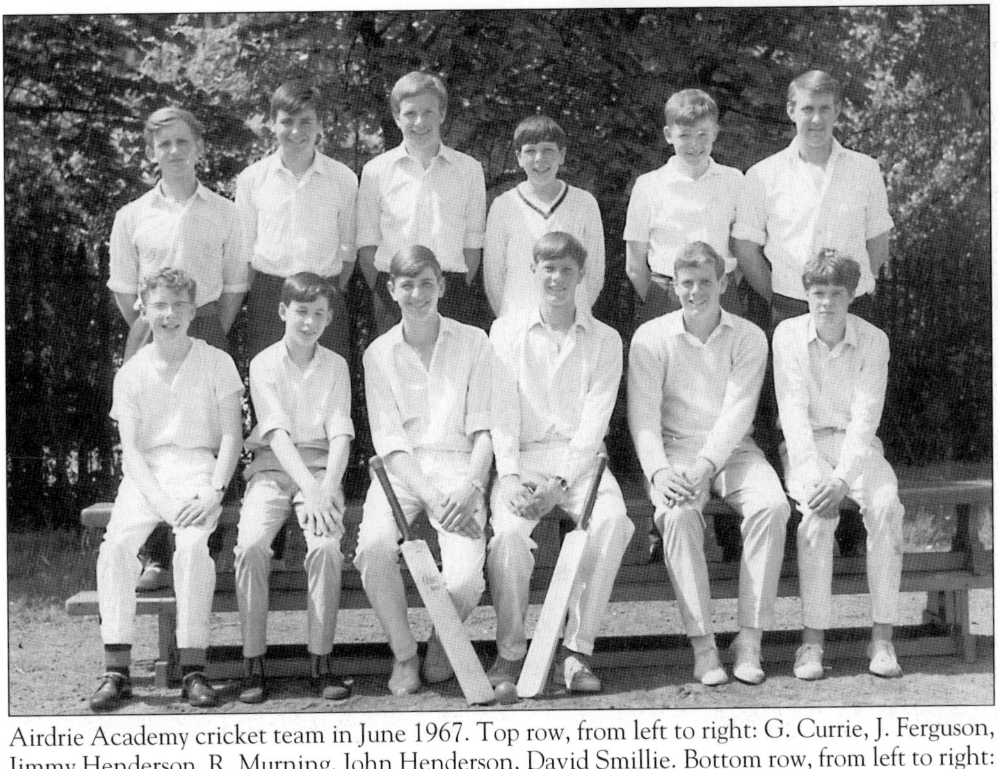

Airdrie Academy cricket team in June 1967. Top row, from left to right: G. Currie, J. Ferguson, Jimmy Henderson, R. Murning, John Henderson, David Smillie. Bottom row, from left to right: Jimmy Rodger, David Cook, Tom Dingwall, Alex Scales, John Sinclair, Ian Scales. (Photograph courtesy John Henderson).

Left: Louise Donoughue, from St Serf's Primary, was the first winner of the Advertiser's Burns Recital Cup, which is sponsored by Whifflet Burns Club. (Photograph courtesy Airdrie & Coatbridge Advertiser).

Right: Airdrie Academy 2nd Juniors Football Team. Top row, from left to right: John Henderson, David Mitchelson, Jim Wilson, Sandy Turnbull, Jim Spiers, Ian Rennie. Bottom row, from left to right: Jim Robertson, Ian Calder, Gavin Lafferty, Billy Cunningham, George Mair, Murray Carr. The teacher is Bill Dalling. (Photograph courtesy John Henderson).

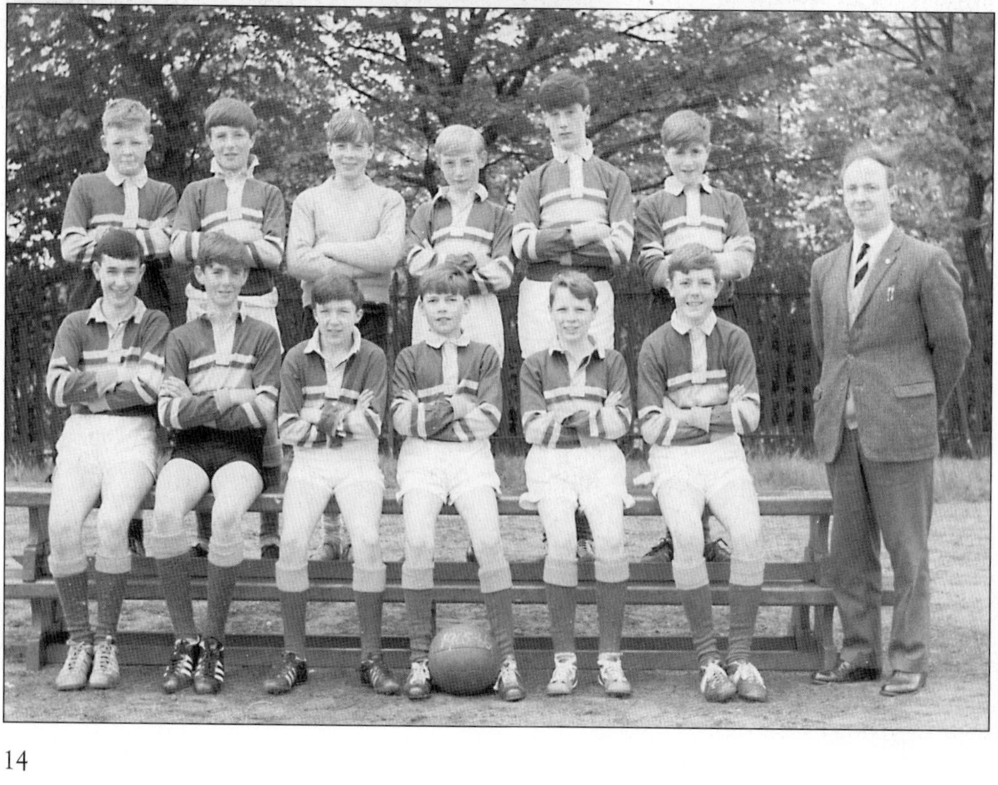

The Third Senior Football Team of 1968 at Airdrie Academy. Top row, from left to right: I. Patterson, C. Frame, Roy Burgess, R. Murning, John Henderson, Ian Shanks. Bottom row, from left to right: E. McPherson, Jim Smillie, Jim Gibson, J. Gallertly, Jim Fleming, John Brown. The teachers are Mr Brown (nick-named 'Paw' Brown) and Mr Russell.

Woodhall Cricket Club, 1971. The club, founded in 1887, was based in Calderbank. It folded after the pavilion was burned down in the 1990s and the club folded as a result. Back row, from left to right: R. Forrester, A.N. Cowan, W. Smith, D.J. McAinish, A. Easton, W. Watt (Hon. Vice President), A. Cunningham, J.R. Henderson, R.B. Forson, D. McKenzie. Front row, from left to right: H. Tart, P. MacLachlan, A.A. Simpson, A.E. Forrester, T. Burn. (Photograph courtesy John Henderson).

Above: Airdrie bowling green in the late Victorian period. (Photograph courtesy Airdrie & Coatbridge Advertiser).

Left: James Cullen, a famous Airdrie pigeon fancier and racer. He came from mining stock in Greengairs and won many cups with his pigeons.

Two

The Diamonds – Airdrieonians FC

The 1902/1903 season Scottish League champions and Lanarkshire Cup winners, the Diamonds were first known as Excelsior Football Club and were founded in 1878. Their first matches were at Mavisbank, which was situated just off Main Street. In 1881 the name was changed to Airdrieonians, a name selected by Tom Forsyth who had a long association with the club. He was involved with Airdrieonians for sixty-one years, a time when he was a goalkeeper and also club chairman twice.

AIRDRIEONIANS FOOTBALL CLUB—Season 1921-22.
Players—Left to Right—Back Row Thom, Drinnan, Price, Dickson, Walker.
2nd Row—Murdoch, Dick, Cornock, Henderson, Gallacher, O'Hagan, Malcolm, Taylor, Allan, Ellis, Preston.
3rd Row—McQueen, Bennie, Hart, Russell, Reid, McCulloch, Doyle, Bradley, Knox.

The team from 1921/1922 and the strip has changed from striped to the diamond design that gives the club its nickname. The diamond strip was first worn against Rangers at Ibrox in August 1912. From left to right, back row: Thom, Drinnan, Dickson, Walker, Second Row: Murdoch, Dick (?) Cornock, Henderson, Gallacher, O'Hagan, Malcolm, Taylor, Allan, Ellis, Preston. Third Row; McQueen, Bennie, Hart, Russell, Reid, McCulloch, Doyle, Bradley, Knox.

A. THOMSON,
AIRDRIEONIANS. F.C.

W. DUNCAN
AIRDRIEONIANS F.C.

D. S. ROMBACH
AIRDRIEONIANS F.C.

Some early players found on cigarette card views. At the turn of the twentieth century cigarette companies gave away free cards with packs and they were avidly collected by both adults and children alike. One of the themes was sports personalities, which even included Airdrie players.

Here are some cards from a set by F&J Smith of Glasgow, issued about 1910-1913.

Ian MacMillan played inside right, he was capped five times for Scotland and was eventually transferred to Rangers.

Bobby Flavell played for the Diamonds in 1946/1947 and went on to play for Hearts and then went to live in South Africa.

William Russell was another star player for the team and is shown here in the 1920s. Russell scored both goals in the 1924 SFA Cup and the team beat Hibernian 2-0. He was transferred to Preston North End and the money used to build a new grandstand which the fans nicknamed the Russell Stand.

An action shot of Airdrie playing against Celtic in 1969 at Broomfield Park. Celtic inside-left Bobby Lennox gets in a shot against Airdrie. Defenders left-back George Caldwell (left) and left-half Derek Whiteford close in.

John Shaw was another famous Diamonds player who played full back and then went on to play for Rangers at Ibrox.

Lawrie Leslie played with the club from 1959-1961.

J. McDougall was another player in the 1924 cup-winning squad.

Derek Whiteford played with the club from 1967 to 1977. He was captain during the 1975 Cup Final when the Airdrieonians were beaten 3-1 by Celtic.

Airdrie play Celtic on 23 August 1969 and Celtic player Willie Wallace (one of the Lisbon Lions) beats Derek Whiteford to the ball.

The Diamonds play Kilmarnock on 6 March 1971. Derek Jarvie is the player shown.

Sandy Clark during a match against Falkirk.

Drew Jarvie played for the team from 1967-1972.

Paul Jonquin holds the record for the number of appearances for the club having played for them from 1961-1979.

Another view of the legendary Paul Jonquin.

The goalkeeper John Martin in a game against Huntly on 19 July 1997.

Airdrie were relegated in 1973 after they were beaten 2-1 by Celtic.

The Airdrie team of 1970. Back row, from left to right: Paul Jonquin, George Caldwell, Roddy McKenzie, Sam Goodwin, Pat Delaney, Derek Whiteford. Front row, from left to right: John Menzies, Billy Watson, Drew Jarvie, Drew Busby, Billy McPheat, Matt Cowan.

The line up prior to the Scottish Cup Final of 1992 when Airdrie were beaten 2-1 by Rangers.

The Airdrie team of 1972 including, back row, from left to right: Chris Mondr, Walter Kidd, Gus Caesar, John Watson, Andy Smith, John Martin, Evan Balfour, Davie Kirkwood, Sammy Conn, Alan Lawrence. Front row, from left to right: Paul Jack, Owen Coyle, Sandy Stewart, Jimmy Sandison, Kenny Black, Jimmy Boyle, Wes Reid.

Airdrieonians moved to Broomfield Park (above) in 1892 and, when the ground was sold to a supermarket chain, they moved again to this state of the art stadium (below) at Shyberry. (Photograph courtesy Airdrie & Coatbridge Advertiser).

Three

Around Airdrie

Commonside Street at the end of the Victorian era.

Market Street around 1900 and the street has been getting dug up ever since.

Alexander Street was named after one of the early residents of Airdrie House and this part of town was developed after the turnpike road from Edinburgh to Glasgow was completed in 1797. As a result of the new road stagecoaches could reach Glasgow in one hour and ten minutes from the town.

The old town hall and the provost at the turn of the twentieth century, Provost Knox.

Hallcraig Street around 1900.

Airdrie leisure centre. (Photograph courtesy Airdrie & Coatbridge Advertiser).

Stirling Street, with Airdrie Savings Bank at the top of the street. (Photograph courtesy Airdrie & Coatbridge Advertiser).

South Bridge Street. (Photograph courtesy Airdrie & Coatbridge Advertiser).

High Street. (Photograph courtesy Airdrie & Coatbridge Advertiser).

Stirling Street. Has that Vauxhall Cavalier on the left been in the wars? (Photograph courtesy Airdrie & Coatbridge Advertiser).

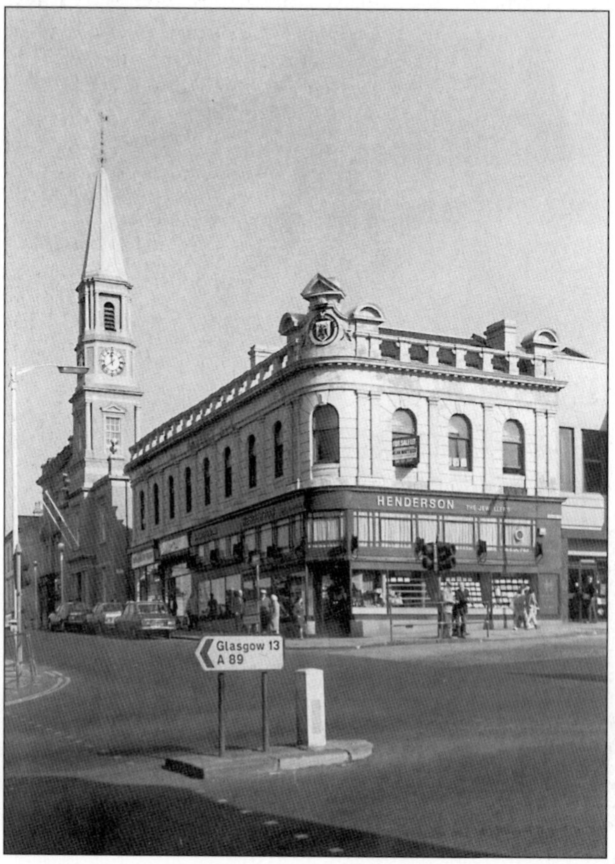

Airdrie Cross. (Photograph courtesy Airdrie & Coatbridge Advertiser).

Arranview was built in 1867 and is one of the two finest villas designed by Alexander 'Greek' Thomson, the other being Holmwood at Cathcart in Glasgow. After the Second World War Arranview was converted to a children's home and its twelve rooms were home to 23 children. By the late 1960s the house had deteriorated and most of the interiors were damaged or destroyed. In 1987 the house was saved by being converted in to flats and the gardens were built over.

Forrest Street. (Photograph courtesy Airdrie & Coatbridge Advertiser).

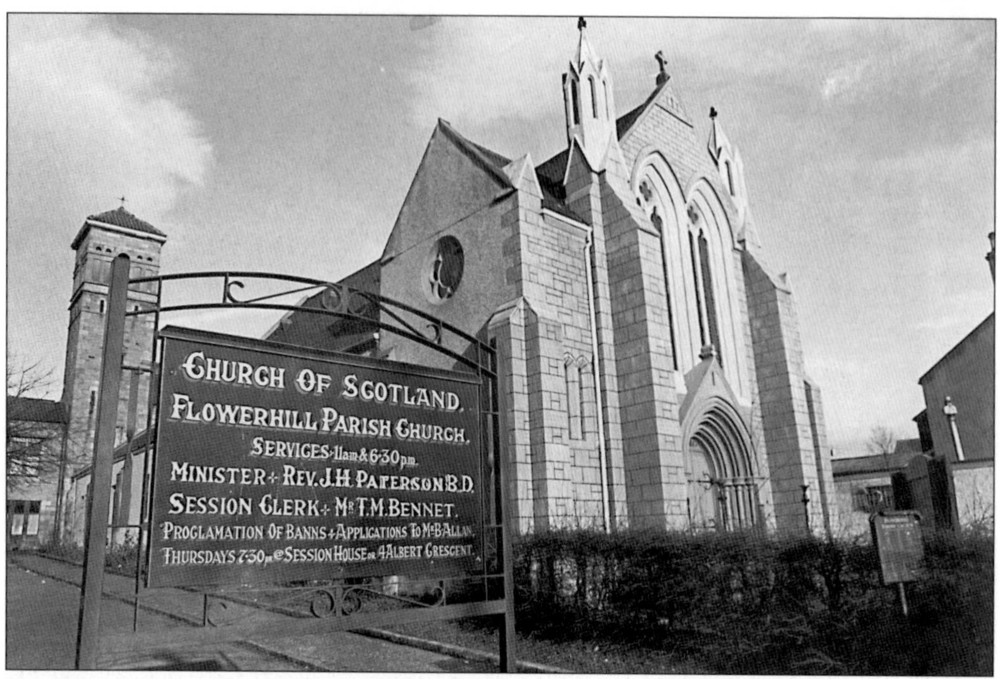

Flowerhill Parish Church. (Photograph courtesy Airdrie & Coatbridge Advertiser).

Clarkston Primary School. (Photograph courtesy Airdrie & Coatbridge Advertiser).

An aerial view of Airdrie. What landmarks can you spot? (Photograph courtesy Airdrie & Coatbridge Advertiser).

Chapleside School is now a resource centre. (Photograph courtesy Airdrie & Coatbridge Advertiser).

This rather poignant view is of the Airdrie War Memorial in memory of those who lost their lives fighting for their country. (Photograph courtesy Airdrie & Coatbridge Advertiser).

The flats at Milton Court – a far cry from the weavers cottages of the eighteenth century. (Photograph courtesy Airdrie & Coatbridge Advertiser).

The Airdrie Savings Bank was instituted on 1 January 1835 and has long been associated with the town. (Photograph courtesy Airdrie & Coatbridge Advertiser).

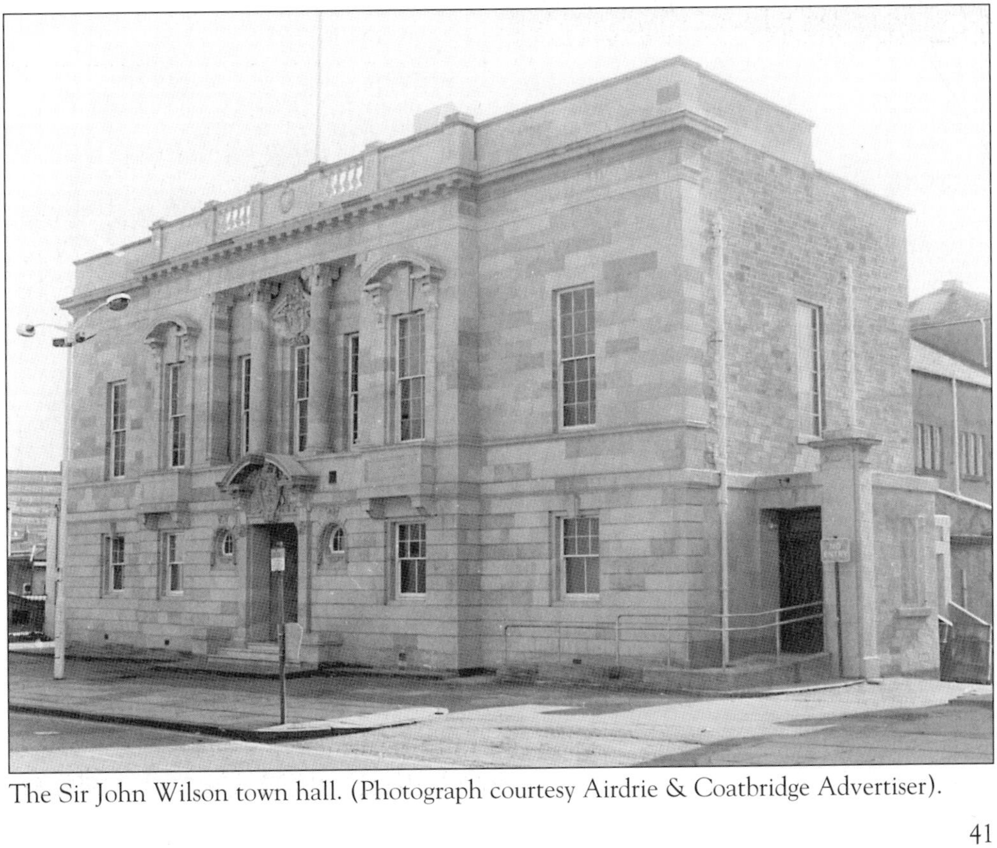

The Sir John Wilson town hall. (Photograph courtesy Airdrie & Coatbridge Advertiser).

A RECRUITING SONG.

Go, and do as they did.

Ev'ry sacred tie that bound him
  To his home at Skeoch Toll,
Pitman snapped when conscience told him,
  That his name should swell the roll
Of those patriotic spirits
  Who for Country took their chance,
At the Dardanelles, or Egypt,
  Or out on the fields of France.

Chorus—

Young men, go, and do as they did,
  Answer Kitchener's appeal,
Ere you'll see your Country's freedom,
  Chrushed beneath the Kaiser's heel.
You befriended, but he hated
  Long before the war broke out,
And his "swelled head" was the outcome
  Of your carelessness, no doubt.

They heard Mother Country calling,
  And, like true sons, they obeyed,
For they could not see her prestige,
  And her reputation fade,
And they rallied round the standard,
  That ensures by land and wave
Full protection to the freeman,
  And sweet freedom to the slave.

Nothing earthly could have kept them
  From responding to the call,
To take part in Britain's glory,
  And with her, to stand or fall.
All that had to life entwined them
  (Let diliquents bear in mind),
To defend Britannia's honour
  They left cheerfully behind.

"Do your share"—says Mother Country;
  "In this crisis, do your share,
Work or fight, and smoothe a wrinkle
  From my honoured brow of care."
If the Allies will be victors,
  This all careless men should know,
That every fit and free man
  In their cause must strike a blow.

WM. MARKHAM BROWN,
3 Davidson's Place, Airdrie.

J. WILLIAMSON.

Four
The Town

Broomknoll Street with the Broomknoll Parish Church on the left. Directly opposite was the Old Airdrie Working Men's Club which was founded in 1869 and based in the High Street. It moved to Broomknoll Street in 1885. The building was extended in 1909-1910 and it has subsequently been demolished. A new club was built on the site and next door is now Lodge St John 166. (Photograph courtesy Airdrie & Coatbridge Advertiser).

Airdrie from the air. (Photograph courtesy Airdrie & Coatbridge Advertiser).

The Airdrie Swimming Pool. (Photograph courtesy Airdrie & Coatbridge Advertiser).

Petersburn library. (Photograph courtesy Airdrie & Coatbridge Advertiser).

'Big Heids' – the piece of installation art at the Eurocentral complex. The industrial complex provides many new jobs for the area to make up for the loss of much of the traditional heavy industry of the town. (Photograph courtesy Airdrie & Coatbridge Advertiser).

Gartlea commercial centre. (Photograph courtesy Airdrie & Coatbridge Advertiser).

Airdrie from the air. (Photograph courtesy Airdrie & Coatbridge Advertiser).

A replica of the *Vulcan*, the world's first iron-hulled ship, which was built in Faskine. The *Vulcan* worked the Forth & Clyde Canal for sixty years and there is a full-size replica of her at the Summerlee Heritage Musuem.

A superb view of the centre of town.

Drumgelloch Station. The village was one of the many mining settlements that sprang up around the town. (Photograph courtesy Airdrie & Coatbridge Advertiser).

The Weaver's Cottages Museum at 23-25 Wellwynd date from 1780 and are the oldest surviving buildings in central Airdrie. It is fitting that these cottages still survive as the original main industry of the town was weaving. The cottages were saved from demolition by Monklands District Council and were renovated by Harley & Murray in 1988-1989. The upper cottage is a reconstruction of a weaver's cottage as it might have been around 1850 and the lower of the two is an exhibition area. No.23 housed in 1861 a total of three families with sixteen persons. (Photograph courtesy Airdrie & Coatbridge Advertiser).

The Car Terminus. First running in February 1904 the Airdrie & Coatbridge Tramways were a great success, carrying about 40,000 people in their first week of operation. In January 1922 the tramway amalgamated with Glasgow Corporation Tramways and an extension from Coatbridge to Baillieston was constructed. A 2d ticket could get you from Ferguslie Mills in Paisley all the way to the terminus in Airdrie. (photograph courtesy Bill Scott)

It is amazing just how much has changed in the seventy years between these two photographs. (Photograph courtesy Airdrie & Coatbridge Advertiser).

Airdrie House and estate originally belonged to the Hamilton family. Robert Hamilton has been referred to as the founder of Airdrie and Sir John Wilson was also a great benefactor to the town. Airdrie House has seen various uses over the years but is probably best known as the district maternity hospital, covering both Airdrie and Coatbridge. It opened as such in 1919 and the house was demolished in 1964, having been vacant for two years. 1971 saw the construction of a new hospital and Monklands District General Hospital opened in 1977.

Airdrie Bowling Club celebrating its centenary in 1952. (Photograph courtesy Airdrie & Coatbridge Advertiser).

Modern Airdrie, with the pedestrian precinct in the middle of town. (Photograph courtesy Airdrie & Coatbridge Advertiser).

Looking west towards Coatbridge and Glasgow.

Looking down from the Cross.

Monklands District General Hospital, built on the site of Airdrie House. (Photograph courtesy Airdrie & Coatbridge Advertiser).

Looking down on to the fire station from the air. (Photograph courtesy Airdrie & Coatbridge Advertiser).

A new building rises at the corner of Wellwynd and Stirling Street. Wellwynd runs down steeply from the High Street to Stirling Street and was once one of Airdrie's notorious wynds. In 1842 the local minister noted that the lodging houses in the street often contained up to fourteen persons per room. The local populace worked in the foundries and engine works in the area and some were also hand loom weavers. (Photograph courtesy Airdrie & Coatbridge Advertiser).

Airdrie's Town House. Construction began in 1824 and the building was completed two years later. The Town House has had numerous uses including a hospital, billets for soldiers and a court room and library. A new clock was added in 1954 after the old one had worn itself out.

At one time there was only one parish church for all of the Monklands and that was the church at Old Monkland. The present church here was built in 1790 but there has been an ecclesiastical settlement here for centuries. In the eighteenth century New Monkland Parish was created and the local churchgoers no longer had to travel to Coatbridge to go to church.

Airdrie Cross at the turn of the twentieth century.

High Street with a distinct lack of transport, sometime in the late 1930s.

South Bridge Street with an abundance of local shops in 1905.

Bank Street, *c*.1906.

Another view of Bank Street around 1905.

Alexander Street and Stirling Street. The centre part of the road with the tramlines was maintained by the tramway company and was often in much better condition than the sides which were maintained by the Burgh Council.

Stirling Street was named not after the town but Andrew Stirling of Drumpellier House who once owned a huge area of land in this part of the town. A view from late 1957

The Cross and Graham Street in 1936.

3.—CLARK STREET, AIRDRIE Craig's Airdrie Series

Clark Street with an open top tram in 1910.

Forest Street, Airdrie (from the West)

Forest Street with another tram visible at the same time.

Victoria Place, Airdrie. At the turn of the twentieth century cycling was a relatively new fad and was a cheap method for many people of seeing the countryside and of commuting to work.

The Public Park has always offered an area of green in amongst the houses and industry of the town.

The New Cross, Airdrie.

Chapel Street's name comes from the Chapel of Ease that stood next to the graveyard. Many of Airdrie's engineering firms were located along Chapel Street. Just some of the local firms noted for their high quality work were John Martin's foundry, the Airdrie Light Engineering Works, Bakery Machine Repairers and Shields & McNicol boilermakers.

Airdrie's war memorial.

King George V and his wife, Queen Mary of Teck, visited the town in July 1914 and here they are outside the Royal Hotel.

A typical postcard of the town from *c*.1940.

The County Buildings were constructed in 1858 and were destroyed by fire in November that year. They were rebuilt and opened one year later. In 1969 they were demolished due to subsidence. Subsidence has been a problem in the area and has been caused by the many ironstone and coal mines underneath the town.

The Market Buildings in 1904. Note the old building with crow-stepped gables in the middle of the photograph.

Taken from the National Bank, this view shows the Cross and Stirling Street in 1936.

The Sir John Wilson Town Hall.

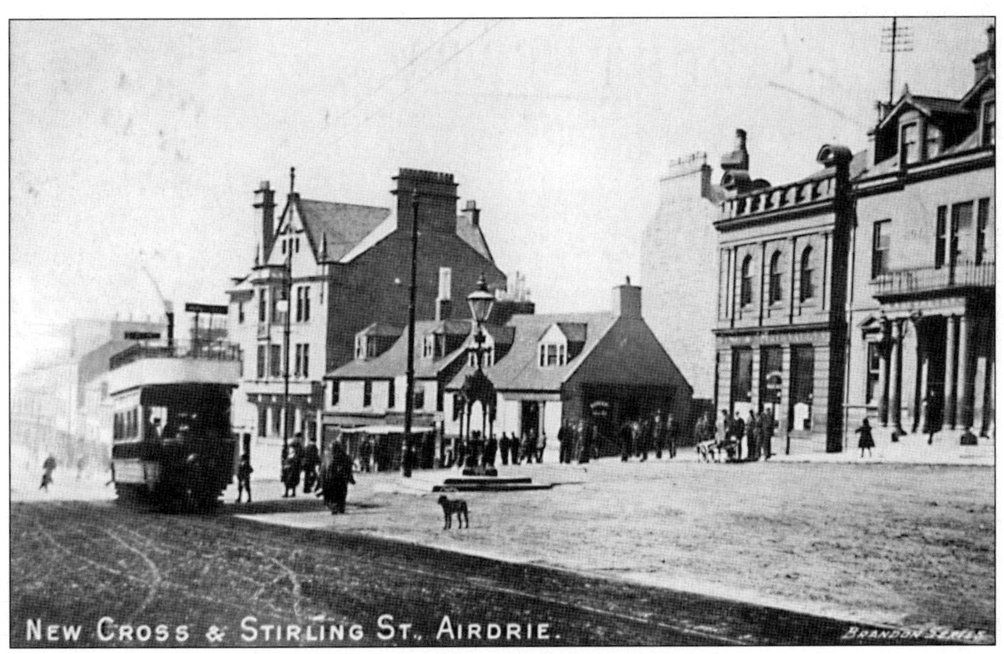

New Cross and Stirling Street soon after the trams were introduced.

Broomknoll Street in 1936.

Airdrie's New Cross sometime in the first decade of the twentieth century.

The Old Cross and High Street around 1910.

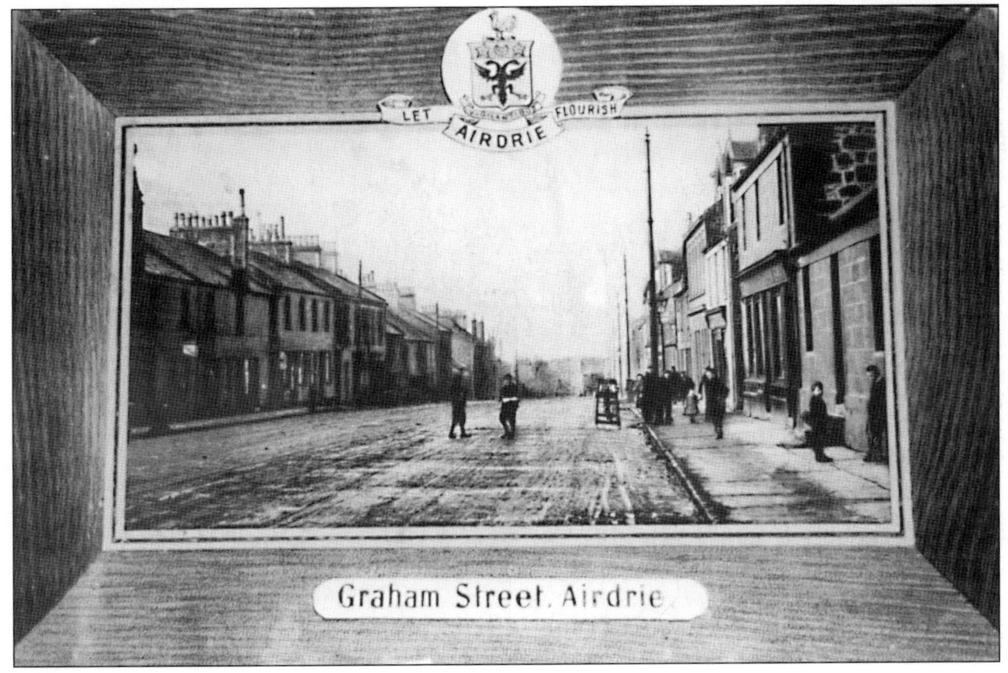

Graham Street on an old postcard view.

The bridge at New Monkland Glen. Once a much loved spot and walk along the banks of the river, this site has changed much over the last hundred years. The old mill visible here has gone and the bridge has been widened to cope with the level of traffic now passing over it. The glen is now sadly neglected.

VIADUCT AND BURN, COATDYKE

The viaduct and burn at Coatdyke at the turn of the twentieth century. The railway line is one of the boundaries between Airdrie and Coatbridge.

A miners' row at Rawyards with Mr and Mrs John Cowen at the door, *c*.1920. Rawyards was at one point the scene of a huge pit disaster. (Photograph courtesy Gina Cowen).

South Bridge Street with Claude Alexander the Scottish Tailors on the right hand side.

Centenary Park in 1936.

Stirling Street sometime about 1900.

Bank Street with the gasworks in the background. The gasworks were situated off Mill Road and were built by the Airdrie Gas Light Company in 1830.

Victoria Place, Airdrie.

The park and bandstand.

The Cross in 1950. How the traffic has changed in fifty years.

South Bridge Street in 1924.

The New Cross.

The Nurses Home.

Airdrie House c.1905.

Forrest Street around 1910.

The Cross in the 1940s.

Graham Street around 1920.

South Bridge Street from the north at the turn of the twentieth century. The horse and cart are parked across the street as it would have had little in the way of brakes. A member of the local constabulary has a drink from the fountain.

The coat of arms of Airdrie.

The public park from the north.

New Cross. This area has now been pedestrianised.

The bazaar, one of Airdrie's shops.

The Cross and Stirling Street, Airdrie.

The Cross and Stirling Street in 1900.

The town hall and swimming baths in 1936.

The fountains at the Old and New Crosses were donated to the town by Provost Forrester and Laird Rankin of Auchengray in 1865. They were made of heavy cast iron and were removed sometime at the turn of the twentieth century.

The Cross and Bank Street. Shops here included James Perman, the tailor, and Bairds. Bairds was actually owned by the Bairds of Gartsherrie who left ironfounding and founded their own shop chain and also owned woollen mills. This view dates from 1961.

South Bridge Street, Airdrie in 1904-1905.

The public park.

Graham Street looking east from the Cross in the 1930s.

Broomknoll Street.

The public park.

Bank Street.

The County Buildings.

The Car Terminus in Forrest Street in the 1960s. Much has changed here over the years.

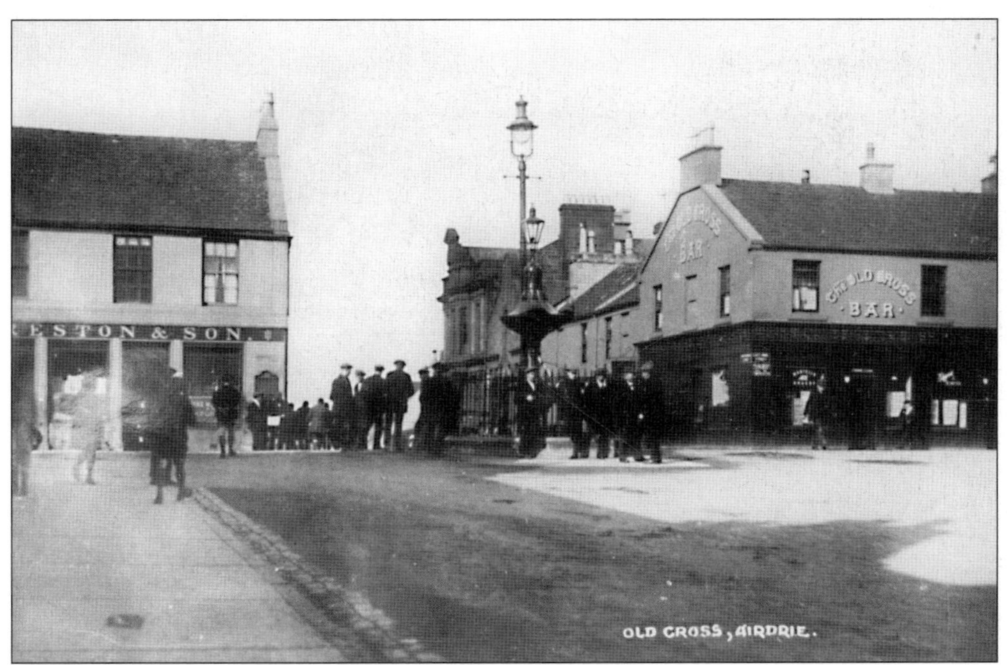

Old Cross has always been a meeting point for folk to chat.

The War Memorial.

A view of the Airdrie Mounted Police from 1904. This postcard was sent on 26 December that year.

Five
Airdrie Boxers

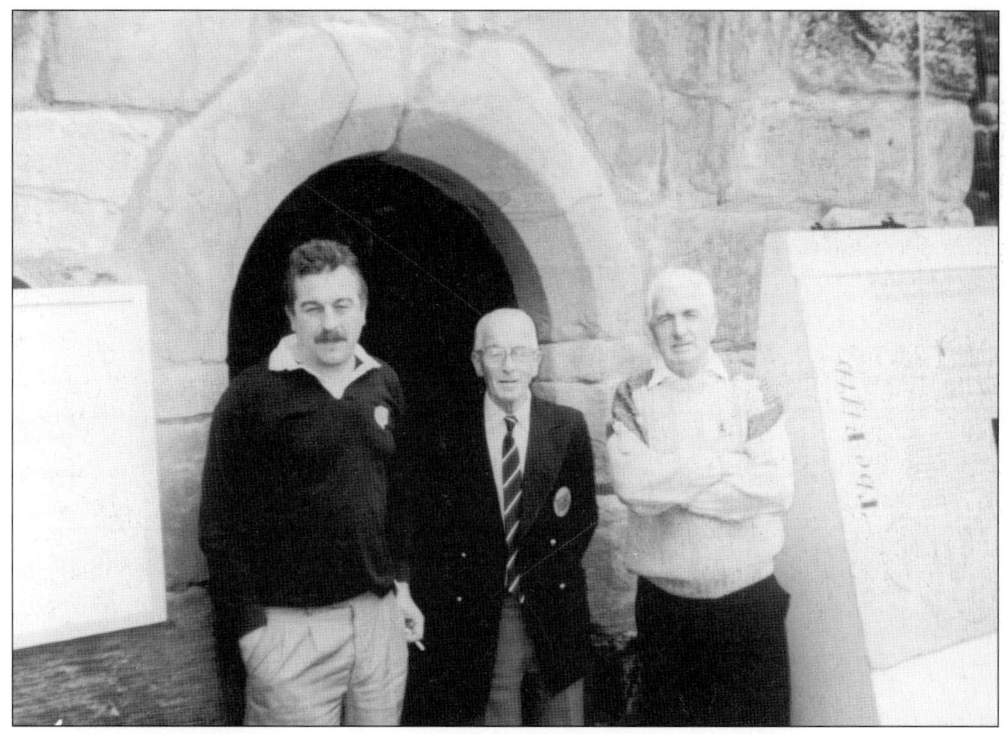

Three members of the famous Lafferty boxing family; from left to right: Percy Lafferty, his father Alex, and Jim Lafferty.

ALEX LAFFERTY

Bantam Champion of Scotland

Song

Napoleon was a fighting man
We all of us admire:
He met his match in Wellington,
Who forced him to retire.
Had "Boney" went to Airdrie
There is not the slightest doubt,
And Lafferty been living
He'd have soon knocked "Boney" out.

CHORUS

For Lafferty has science, that's what all sportsmen say,
He knows the Noble Art of hit, and stop, and get away,
He has never been defeated, all admire his style and pluck,
Some think he carries a horse shoe in his boxing glove, for luck

A lick from *Alec* Lafferty -
He's got a healthy punch -
Makes some good men *throw up* the sponge
And some *throw up* their lunch.
He'll paint your eye with pleasure,
Knock the whiskers off your cheek,
And you won't require to go and see
A Barber for a week.

Unlike some boxers, Lafferty
Is always clean and straight;
He's open now to make a match,
With anything his weight.
He'll stand up to you gamely,
Let you punch him black and blue,
And just to show his friendship
He will do as much for you.

Poem

Don't talk about battles terrific.
If I like to speak, it's me can,
When speaking of lads scientific,
Well - Airdrie's Bantam's the man.
His style and his smile it is pleasing,
His head he can always keep cool,
They like him, I'll tell you the reason:
His hit's like the kick of a mule,
He'll put you to sleep while you're waiting,
He'll rub all the skin off your snout,
And now I'll be after relating
A few of the nuts he's knocked out;
In five rounds Young Currie of Bellshill
Was quietly sent to repose:
Jim Martin, Coatbridge, lasted eight rounds
Then dropped through a whack on the nose;
Jack Reynolds, Jim Easton, Matt Sweenie,
Young Lafferty knocked them out flat;
Joe Easterman, London, stood two rounds
Then woke up and enquired for his hat,
Curley Osborne of London he knocked out,
And hammered his man like a drum;
Then one night before taking his supper,
He knocked out Bill Phelin of "Brum";
Calderbank sent out Jim Brannen,
Tom Hendry came from Belfast;
The Calderbank hero stood five rounds,
The Belfast man's first, was his last.
All Lafferty's wins I can't mention -
There's not enough paper I vow,
If wanting a fight's your intention,
Alec Lafferty's open just now.
I don't need to speak of our Bantam,
All Airdrie is proud of the lad,
When you meet him don't think you've a soft thing,
Because if you do, you'll be had.

Price. - - ONE PENNY

A song and poem about Alex Lafferty, one time bantam-weight boxing champion of Scotland.

Jem Lafferty, the first of the Lafferty boxing clan. Jem was a bare knuckle featherweight champion boxer and as an amateur won a bantam weight championship In New York at the New York Athletic Club. This is Jem after his return from New York c.1897 wearing the belt he won in the USA. Jem died on 24 April 1924.

Jem Lafferty senior with his son Percy and Mick Riley in 1920. Mick helped Jem found the Monklands Boxing Club.

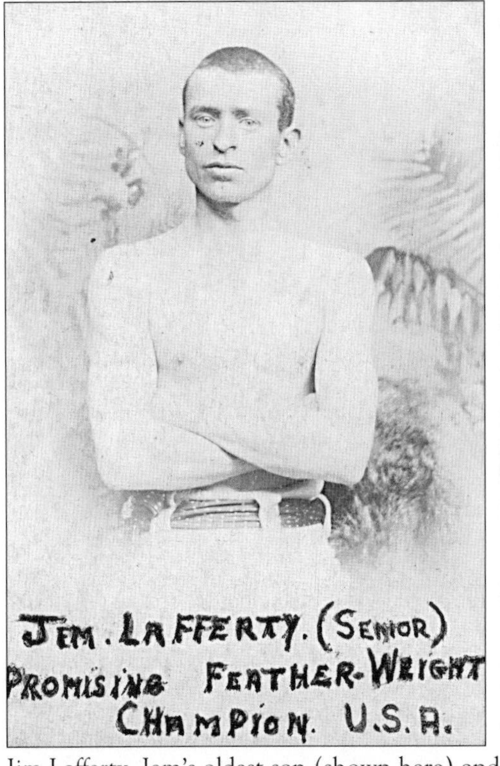

JEM . LAFFERTY. (SENIOR)
PROMISING FEATHER-WEIGHT
CHAMPION. U.S.A.

Jim Lafferty, Jem's oldest son (shown here) and his brothers, Alex, Johnny and Percy, were all trained and managed by Jem. This view dates from 1910.

Alex Lafferty was the best known of the brothers and by the tender age of seventeen he was challenging any boxer at 7 stone 7 pounds for £50 and his title.

Alex lafferty went to fight for his country and is shown here at home in 1917 recoverfing from his wounds. He returned to France and was killed in action on 14 April 1918. He left a wife, Mary, and four young children.

Alex and John Lafferty at an exhibition match in Whiterigg in 1908. Their father, jem, is referee and Alex is on the right.

15 Rounds Draw with Jas. Easton, Glasgow, for Flyweight Championship.
16 Rounds Draw with Peter Bannochan, Glasgow
6 Rounds Draw with Jim M'Culloch, Belfast
Beat Jack M'Quade, Glasgow, in 10 rounds
Beat Chris. Harrison, Blantyre, in 10 rounds
Knocked out Paddy Lee, Dublin, in 3 rounds
Beat Arthur Cunningham, Holytown, in 10 rounds
Beat Archie Nicol, Glasgow, in 6 rounds
Beat Jack Thornton, Glasgow, in 6 rounds
Beat Young M'Quade, Glasgow in 6 rounds
Knocked out Tom M'Iver, Calderbank, in 9 rounds
Knocked out Joe Harrison, Blantyre, in 5 rounds
Beat Peter Bannochan, Glasgow, in 4 rounds
Knocked out Young Currie, Bellshill, in 5 rounds
Knocked out Jim Martin, Coatbridge, in 8 rounds
Knocked out Jack Reynolds, Castlecary, in 8 rounds
Knocked out Jim Easton, Glasgow, in 5 rounds
Knocked out Jim Mason, Coatbridge, in 7 rounds
Knocked out Jim M'Culloch, Belfast, in 7 rounds
Knocked out Mat Sweenie, Glasgow, in 6 rounds
Knocked out Joe Easterman, London, in 2 rounds
Knocked out Jim M'Ilwraith, Belfast, in 2 rounds
Knocked out Jack Docherty, Glasgow, in 2 rounds
Knocked out Billy Nelson, Glasgow, in 1 round
Knocked out Billy Harrison, West Hartlepool, in 3 rounds
Knocked out Jack Thornton, Glasgow, in 2 rounds
Knocked out Ernie Goodwin, Birmingham, in [illegible]
[illegible] Donnelly, Newcastle, in 10 rounds
Knocked out Curly Osborne, London, in 5 rounds
Knocked out Bill Phelin, Birmingham, in 4 rounds
Knocked out Jim Brannen, Calderbank, in 5 rounds
Knocked out Tom Hendry, Belfast, in 1 round
Knocked out Dan Higgins, Newcastle, in 8 rounds
Knocked out Peter Thomson, Sheffield, in 7 rounds
Beat Young Edge, Birkenhead, in 10 and 20 rounds
Knocked out Sammy Wright, Belfast, in 7 rounds
Knocked out Young Doyle, Manchester, in 6 rounds
Knocked out Albert Cocksedge, Leicester, in 6 rounds
Drew with Ralph Marshall, Glasgow, 20 rounds
Knocked out Young Dominick, Leeds, in 5 rounds
Beat Jack Simms, Leeds, in 15 rounds
Knocked out Tommy Fishburn, W. Hartlepool, 6 rounds
Knocked out Harry Brodigan, Manchester, in 3 rounds
Knocked out Fred Anderson, London, in 2 rounds
Knocked out Peter Cullen, Dublin, in 4 rounds
Beat Sid. Smith, London, 20 rounds
Knocked out Bill Hughes, Newcastle, in 5 rounds
Beat Johnnie Hepburn, Greenock, in 10 rounds
Beat Munro Grainger, Freddy Welsh's partner, in 10 rounds
Claimed forfeit of £10 from Sid. Smith
Beat Nicky Kelly, Newcastle, 20 rounds
Beat Nicky Kelly, Newcastle, 10 rounds
Knocked out Harry Foster, Baillieston, 1 round
Beat Young Fox, Leeds, 20 rounds

ALEX. LAFFERTY'S RECORD.

BRITISH AND AMERICAN.

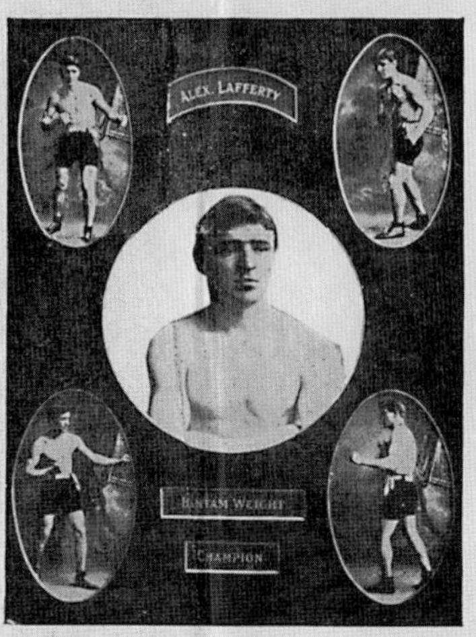

Beat Billy Green, Chesterfield, 10 rounds
Knocked out Jack Brown, Sheffield, 5 rounds
Beat Johnny M'Guire, Belfast, 10 rounds
Lost on points (Londsdale Belt) to Digger Stanley, 20 rounds
Knocked out Rags Johnstone, Newcastle, 5 rounds
Beat Frank Warner, 20 rounds
Beat Bat. M'Carthy, Cardiff, 20 rounds
Beat Frank Warner, London, 15 rounds
Knocked out Bat. M'Carthy, Cardiff, 14 rounds
Knocked out Kid Driscoll, Keighley 5 rounds
Knocked out George Hobbs, Huddersfield, 7 rounds
Knocked out Fred Hartley, Dewsbury, 5 rounds
Knocked out Robertson Lindsay, Belfast, 4 rounds
Knocked out Sammy Kellar, London, 13 rounds
Knocked out Myer Stringer, Glasgow, 15 rounds
Beat Nat. Brooks, London, on points, 20 rounds
Knocked out Billy Dean, Dublin, 8 rounds
Knocked out Pte. James, Sheffield, 2 rounds
Knocked out Tancy Lee, Edinburgh, for the Bantam-Weight Championship, 13 rounds
Beat Young Fox, Leeds, 15 rounds
Lost Young Fox, London, 20 rounds
Knocked out Curley Hughes, Hamilton, 1 round
Knocked out Fred Sydney, Newcastle, 9 rounds
Beat Tom Distillion, Liverpool, 15 rounds
Knocked out Alf Wye, London, 2 rounds
Beat Johnnie Best, Glasgow, 20 rounds
Beat Ernie Goodwin, Birmingham, 10 rounds
Beat Tom Distillion, France, 20 rounds
Lost Curley Walker London, 20 rounds
Beat Fred Jones, London, 15 rounds
Drew Billy Benyon, Liverpool, 15 rounds
Knocked out Fred Niven, 13 rounds, for Featherweight Championship
Drew Tommy Harrison, Liverpool, 15 rounds
Knocked out Johnnie M'Guire, Belfast, 14 rounds
Beat Nat. Brooks, 7 rounds
Knocked out Billy Deans, Dublin, 1 round
Beat Driver Wintles, Essex, 4 rounds
Knocked out Pte. Johnstone, Colchester, in 1 round
Drew Chick Wallace, Dundee, 6 rounds
Beat 6 men for the Div. Lightweight Championship, France
Beat Cpl. Taylor, Australia, 10 rounds, France

Knocked out Charley Burns, Brooklyn, 5 rounds
Knocked out Young Packy M'Farlane, Brooklyn, 4 rounds
Beat Kid Goodman, Brooklyn, 6 rounds
Beat Eddie Sherman, Brooklyn, 10 rounds
Beat Mick Carrol, New York, 10 rounds
Beat Kid Goodman, New York, 10 rounds
Beat Fighting Fitzpatrick, Brooklyn, 10 rounds
Knocked out Artie Edwards, New York, 10 rounds
Beat Battling Lahn, New York, 10 rounds
Knocked out Young Ketchell, New York, 2 rounds

Memo from ALEX. LAFFERTY,

BANTAM AND FEATHERWEIGHT CHAMPION OF SCOTLAND.

Alex Lafferty's impressive boxing record. Soon after his death some of his friends held a Benefit boxing match for his family which helped raise money for a memorial stone in New Monkland graveyard.

Alex was born at 42 Wellwynd on 10 February 1889 and began boxing professionally in 1907. His career was triumphant until his untimely death in 1918 and he was the first Scot to box for a Lonsdale belt. In 1911 he beat Tancy Lee to win the Scottish Bantamweight title and was beaten in points by Digger Stanley in 1912 after a gruelling twenty rounds. In 1914 he went to America and took on many boxers there. At the start of the war he returned to Scotland and joined the Royal Engineers.

Alex Lafferty in 1912 just before he took on Digger Stanley for the Lonsdale Belt.

Alex recovering from his wounds in 1917 when he was injured fighting the Germans.

A 1960 photograph of Monkland Boxing Club at Glengowan School garden fete. Back row, from left to right: A. Livingstone (youth trainer), W. McHugh (assistant trainer), Jim Lafferty (club coach), Alex Lafferty (club manager), Jim Wright (club secretary). Middle row, left to right: Percy Lafferty, A. Cameron, L. Kelly, J. Smith, W. McHugh Jnr, J. McHugh, J. Burns, A. Smith. Front row, left to right: J. McGowan, A. Cameron. The medals on display were won by the lads in the 1960 season.

Monkland Boxing Club boxers on 21 January 1965. Back row, from left to right: J. Smith, J. Cunningham, T. Menzies, I. Wotherspoon, T. Henderson. Front row, from left to right: A. Livingstone (trainer), M. Gracie, J. Lafferty (secretary), P. Lafferty, A. Lafferty (club president).